C000108036

1 MONTH OF
FREE
READING

at

www.ForgottenBooks.com

By purchasing this book you are eligible for one month membership to ForgottenBooks.com, giving you unlimited access to our entire collection of over 1,000,000 titles via our web site and mobile apps.

To claim your free month visit:

www.forgottenbooks.com/free689057

* Offer is valid for 45 days from date of purchase. Terms and conditions apply.

ISBN 978-0-483-95668-1
PIBN 10689057

This book is a reproduction of an important historical work. Forgotten Books uses
state-of-the-art technology to digitally reconstruct the work, preserving the original format
whilst repairing imperfections present in the aged copy. In rare cases, an imperfection in
the original, such as a blemish or missing page, may be replicated in our edition. We do,
however, repair the vast majority of imperfections successfully; any imperfections that
remain are intentionally left to preserve the state of such historical works.

Forgotten Books is a registered trademark of FB &c Ltd.
Copyright © 2018 FB &c Ltd.
FB &c Ltd, Dalton House, 60 Windsor Avenue, London, SW19 2RR.
Company number 08720141. Registered in England and Wales.

For support please visit www.forgottenbooks.com

JANUARY 9, 1925

The ᴀMERICAN ʟEGION Weekly

10c
a Copy

January 9, 1925

The AMERICAN LEGION Weekly

Vol. 7, No. 2

Table of Contents

The American Legion Weekly is the official publication of The American Legion and The American Legion Auxiliary and is owned exclusively by The American Legion. Copyright, 1924, by the Legion Publishing Corporation. Published weekly at Indianapolis, Ind. Entered as second class matter March 24, 1920, at the Post Office at New York, N. Y., under act of March 3, 1879. Application for transfer of second class privilege from New York, N. Y., to Indianapolis, Ind., pending. Price $1.50 the year. Acceptance for mailing at special rate of postage provided for in Section 1103, Act of October 3, 1917, authorized March 31, 1921.

Publication Office, Indianapolis, Ind.

Advertising Office, 331 Madison Avenue, New York City; Western Advertising Office, 22 West Monroe Street, Chicago

JACK O'DONNELL's account of the prevalence of race-track gambling in this country, reminds us of the only time we put money on a horse (the amount was two dollars, for in that day the Government was still publishing two-dollar bills and we wanted to get rid of one, and also to say that we had once placed a real bet with a real bookmaker on a real horse and then quit). The horse's name was Puritan, or Pilgrim, or Cotton Mather, or something associated with early New England history, but he must have stumbled over Plymouth Rock, because while the track record was broken in the same race, this feat was accomplished with another horse.

* * *

WE ARE always looking for trouble, and we are all set right now to have somebody write in: "Why in blazes is the Weekly running a story about bookmakers and gambling?" Right away we admit that there are more important (and duller) subjects. And immediately afterward we want to add that any social phenomenon, whether it is gambling or politics or chewing gum or moving pictures or co-operative marketing or cross-word puzzles, that affects as many as five million citizens (and that's Mr. O'Donnell's estimate of the number of men and women who bet on a horse at least once a year) is of definite social and historical importance to us all no matter how we feel about gambling. That's not an apology—it's a statement.

* * *

SPEAKING of gambling, there is a reference on page 6 to the conservatism of Frank Samuel of the Legion's National Headquarters at the poker table. It is intimated that Mr. Samuel drops his hand with a sigh, regardless of the size of the pot, when confronted with the problem of catching a ten to fit in between a nine and a jack. But what does Mr. Samuel do with a three flush? If he's at all like us he throws down his hand, unless there's real money up, say once in eighty-two years. To our mind the most desperate form of poker radicalism is the attempt to swell a three flush into the real thing. We admit we have seen it accomplished once or twice to our own detriment. But the men who filled thereby acquired the three-flush habit for life, and forever after were suckers ripe for plucking.

MR. SAMUEL displays an equally sound conservatism toward prophesying definite increases in Legion membership. Therefore, when he is hopeful the rest of us may safely borrow his sentiments. And there isn't any question of prophecy when it comes down to the figures already totaled up. Never before at this early day in a new year has the Legion been in such a flourishing condition. That's not prophecy, it's cold arithmetic. It represents not birds in the bush but birds in the posts.

* * *

HERE'S some more arithmetic: Turn to the story of the paper-selling campaign put on every year by Brackenridge (Pennsylvania) Post—it's on page 7. You'll see that the post makes $800 a year by this plan. Suppose every one of the more than 11,000 posts in the Legion embarked on the same enterprise. Doubtless it couldn't be done—not every town has a paper mill as Brackenridge has—but assuming, for theoretical purposes, that it could be done, it would mean nearly $9,000,000 in revenue for local posts every year. Nine million dollars is a whole lot—and think of the good it could do!

Bookmakers watching a race at an Eastern track after all bets have been placed. The picture is of 1902 vintage. Note the tricky derby worn by the well-dressed man of that day, if race track gentlemen's top-pieces were any criterion. Styles have changed since then, but bookies and their public have not

It's *a* Shame
to Take *the* Money

By JACK O'DONNELL

IN the local room of the Boston newspaper where she works she is called the Mouse. This because she is so quiet, so reserved, so colorless. She comes and goes, but she's always seen before she's heard. That's the way of a lady, according to the copy books.

One day recently the Mouse noiselessly approached the sporting editor. "I hear you are winning a lot of money betting on the races," she said in her low, toneless voice. "I'd like to make some extra money. Will you wager this for me on the next horse you bet on?"

Then she slipped a ten-dollar bill into the hand of the amazed sporting editor. The Mouse is one of the five million men and women in the United States who, at least once a year, bet on the races. If she gives that sporting editor ten dollars to wager five or six times a year she is one of the two and a half million who bet occasionally. If she gives him ten dollars, or any other sum, to bet five or six times a week she is one of the million men and women who bet regularly.

Every day that the ponies run, whether in the United States, Canada, Mexico or Cuba, followers of the bang-tails in this country wager between $2,500,000 and $5,000,000, according to Roi Tolleson, one of the greatest students of horse racing in America, and a recognized authority in the art of picking winners. Tolleson has been owner and trainer of race horses, bookmaker, player, handicapper and writer on turf subjects all of his adult life. He demonstrated his uncanny knowledge of horses back in 1921 when he became the sensation of Broadway by giving readers of his racing papers so many winners that they ruined hundreds of bookmakers in Greater New York.

Tolleson estimates that thirty million admissions are paid to race tracks in the United States, Canada, Mexico and Cuba in a single year.

"Horse racing no longer is the sport of kings," he told me. "It is the sport of the common people. It has a greater drawing power than baseball, football or prize fighting., The largest crowd of fight followers ever gathered together attended the Dempsey-Carpentier fight at Jersey City a few years ago. They numbered ninety thousand. A thrilling world series game draws less than eighty thousand on its biggest day. Less than eighty thousand persons witnessed the Yale-Harvard football game a year ago last fall, and thousands fewer last fall when it poured all through the game. Yet a hundred thousand men and women were present at Churchill Downs, Kentucky, last May 17th when Black Gold won the Kentucky Derby."

"What is the magnet that attracts such great crowds to racing?" I asked. "Is it the average person's love of outdoor sports?"

"Hardly!" he laughed. "It's the larceny that's in every man's heart to a greater or lesser degree. It is the desire to beat the other fellow in a speculative transaction—the same desire that grips the bookmaker, the stock broker, the Wall Street gambler, the card player, the oil-stock and real-estate speculator.

"If I asked you to change a ten dollar bill for me and you gave me back eleven dollars by mistake and I said nothing about it I'd be a thief. But if, after counting the money, I said to you, 'I'll bet you five dollars you made a mistake in counting this money,' and you felt so sure you hadn't that you'd accept the bet, I'd be committing petty larceny because I'd be betting on a sure thing, justifying my action by telling myself that you had the privilege of refusing the wager.

"When a man bets on a horse race, accepting three to one from a bookmaker, he does so believing he has the best of the bet. Otherwise he'd be a fool to bet, wouldn't he? That's where the larceny comes in. The bookmaker, on the other hand, wouldn't lay three to one unless he felt sure he had the best end of it. That's where the larceny in his heart creeps out.

"Vanity is another thing that makes bettors," he continued. "The average man or woman is highly pleased with himself when he or she out-smarts another, especially when that other is a professional gambler."

In an effort to find out who plays the races I went to one of the biggest bookmakers in New York, the head of a bookmaking syndicate that handles millions of dollars annually.

"Who bet on the races?" He repeated my question. "Everybody. That is, men and women from all walks of life—brokers, beggars, bankers, laborers, doctors, dentists, actors—good and bad—bootblacks, judges, chorus girls, waiters, housewives, manicures, streetcar conductors, gamblers, reformers, authors, thieves, artists—everybody!

"RECENTLY a new class of players has sprung up. They are what we call the funnies. They are the players who follow the tips given out by the cartoon tipsters in the daily newspapers. These players are chiefly stenographers, shop girls and clerks. They see two funny fellows in a cartoon trying to pick winners day after day. Everybody is talking about them. Then two stenographers will pool their pin money—or their lunch money—and make a bet on the funny chap's selection. If the horse picked by the cartoon tipster wins these girls will get back perhaps two or three dollars for the one dollar they bet.

"That hooks them. Immediately they begin asking, 'How long has this game been going on?' They tell their friends about the easy money they picked up. That gets more recruits. All join the army of small bettors which springs up every year. Eventually some of these small bettors become big bettors. Every plunger the turf has ever known was at the beginning a piker. Pittsburgh Phil's first wager was a half dollar, it's said. He became known as the greatest plunger of all time. He won and lost half a dozen fortunes. He died with a $2,000,-000 bankroll."

"What percentage of players win?" I asked.

"One in fifty. Those that win consistently are men and women who make horse racing a life work. They are the sharpshooters of the turf. They did not start out deliberately to make a living by betting on horses, but two out of every hundred become obsessed with the idea they can eventually win, and they stick, suffering the stings of fortune for two, three or four years. Eventually they learn enough about the game to beat it, or they become bookmakers, realizing that, after all, the bookmaker has all the best of it.

"I have a man who has been playing with me twelve years. He has been a consistent winner for nine of the twelve.

He is an office man, receiving a salary of a hundred dollars a week. But he is an automaton. The automatons are the ones that beat the races. They do not depend upon their own judgment of a horse. They learned not to do that during the years they were learning the game. They subscribe for three or four of the best racing papers published—papers that specialize in turf news and information about horses in training. These papers employ expert handicappers who make selections of the probable winners on a day's card.

"The automatons watch these handicappers, keeping tabs on the number of winners they pick. Then they follow the four leading experts. When these four handicappers, each of whom uses a different method of picking the horse most likely to win a given race, agree upon the same horse or horses the automatons bet on that horse or those horses. The players who follow this system of betting never make a wager on a horse unless all four experts pick it to win. Sometimes they play two or three races a day, sometimes none at all. Sometimes these horses win, but not always.

"In New York there are three publications which specialize on last-minute information. These papers give scratches, names of jockeys that are to ride, selections made by their own handicappers and also the selections made by the high-priced tipsters who sell tips on one horse or more a day to their clients for sums ranging from one dollar to a hundred. One of these papers actually dominates the betting market because the sharpshooters follow the selections made by its handicappers. When four of them agree upon one horse the automatons send in their checks. If the four select a certain horse to win a certain race and that horse opens at four to one it is almost sure to be bet so heavily that the closing price will be two to one or even less.

"IN ONE respect at least the followers of these expert handicappers have it on the bookmakers. They have four experts working for them while we have only one. Our one man hands us his choices, picked on past performances, workouts, weights, jockeys, post positions and other information which he picks up around the track. The bookmakers' prices are based on his judgment. If he makes an error and selects as the probable winner a horse that should be second or third choice the price on the probable winner selected by the four experts is bound to be comparatively long. But it doesn't stay that way for any length of time. The sharpshooters—the wise automatons who have four experts working for them—bet on the logical winner and drive the price down. They realize that we have made a bad guess—made a false favorite."

"What about the tipsters who advertise so extensively in the racing papers?" I asked.

"Some are good, some are bad, and some are just plain crooks. There are some hard-working, well-intentioned men among them—men who have studied the racing game and who do their utmost to give their clients winners. These are the attorneys of the turf. Their sell their tips just as a lawyer

sells legal advice. The best of them are aids to the newcomers to the racing game and to the hundreds of thousands of men and women who go to the races only once or twice a year and who don't bother their heads or know anything about past performances. To this large class the professional tipster gives the best information he can, based on years of study of thoroughbreds, handicapping knowledge, and other information. Certainly, the man or woman who plays this information stands a better chance of winning than the novice who goes to the track and bets on a horse because it has a pretty name, or because the colors worn by the jockey please the fancy of the player."

WHEN this bookmaker told me that hundreds of thousands of year-round bettors were to be found in the small cities and towns of the country, that a great majority of them never saw a rack track or a race horse, and that the majority of these were "information players," I decided to check up on him. I picked out a small, typical American city in Ohio—a town I happened to know well—to investigate. I knew a chap there who had been a waiter in the leading hotel back in 1917. In those days he was a two-bit player. A two-dollar bet was a plunge for him. I didn't find this chap at the hotel. He's in business now, drives a car and is a pillar of the church of his choice. Hearing this I figured, of course, that he no longer played the races. I went around to his place of business to call. At the very moment I entered he was at the telephone. "Two hundred across the board!" he was saying to the man at the other end of the wire—a bookmaker in Columbus, fifty miles away.

This ex-waiter told me later that he had bet six hundred dollars on a horse on which he had a tip for which he had paid a nationally known tipster a hundred dollars. Incidentally, that horse ran second. Four others that he had bought and paid for that week had failed to get down in front, two running second and two being unplaced.

In the half hour I spent in this place a printer, an insurance agent, a bootblack, a clothing-house manager, two waiters, a druggist, a furniture dealer and an auto accessories dealer came in and telephoned bets to bookmakers at Columbus, Dayton and Cincinnati. The bookmakers, I was told, paid the tolls on these long-distance calls. After each race the former waiter called one of the bookmakers and got the name of the winner of the previous race and the odds on the horses in the next race, together with the names of the jockeys and the post positions of the runners.

All of these players were regulars, yet none of them ever went to the race tracks more than once a year. All but two or three had been at Churchill Downs, two hundred and fifty miles away, to see the Kentucky Derby. All followed the professional handicappers and none depended entirely on his own figures in making choices. They bought information from professional tipsters just as you or I would buy legal advice from an attorney if we were going to organize a stock company or make a will. But none of them was a winner

(Continued on page 14)

They Beat *the* Forty-Niners *by* Four Thousand Years

These trees in the Giant Forest of Sequoia National Park in the Sierras of California were lusty saplings when Rome's great rival, Carthage, was a boom town. They are now under the protection of Visalia Post of The American Legion, which each year travels sixty miles from its valley home to the grove on the mountain slope, where it initiates new Legionnaires

THEY are now digging the skeleton of Carthage out of the sands of the African desert which have covered it for several thousand years, and they are trying to read the history of the dead city in its bones and buried walls. Carthage, so old that only a few legends now hint of its once marvelous glory and only a few of its legendary kings and heroes have come down to us by name!

But on the eastern slope of the Sierras in California there is a living contemporary of the dead Carthage, a Brobdingnagian tree thirty-six and a half feet from bark to bark on a line measured through its heart and 280 feet high. It is the General Sherman Tree—five thousand years old, perhaps—one of the thousands of giant sequoias, whose average diameter is ten feet, which compose the Giant Forest. Perhaps at this moment it rises skyward from banks of driven snow. As it stands thus in winter majesty and solitude it is still a symbol of the beauty which The American Legion in California has pledged itself to preserve. It stands for all the giant sequoias and the redwoods of the State of California which are under the guardianship of the scores of California Legion posts.

When the San Francisco National Convention of The American Legion in 1923 adopted a resolution calling on the people of the entire nation to fight against the destruction of the redwoods of Humboldt County, Cali-

The initiation ceremony in the shadows of the Giant Forest

fornia, its action was but one development in a movement which has been gathering strength in California for several years with American Legion support.

Humboldt County is on the California coast and the border of Oregon. The fight to save the redwood trees from being sawed into logs goes on. Meanwhile, safe in one of Uncle Sam's national preserves—the Giant Forest, in middle western California—the sequoias bid defiance to man and the elements while the Legion posts of Tulare County make shrines in their groves. Visalia Post, whose home is the town of Visalia, is the leader in a movement to make the Sequoia National Park the great outing center of California summers. As the post meets these winter evenings in its comfortable clubhouse in Visalia, sixty miles from the forest, it makes plans to hold next summer—on July 4th probably—a huge rally in the Giant Forest, to be attended not only by the Legionnaires of all that section of California but by thousands of other *(Continued on page 14)*

Signs *That* Point *the* Way
to the Legion's Biggest Year

FRANK SAMUEL, of Kansas, is Director of the Organization and Membership Division at National Headquarters of The American Legion.

Mr. Samuel has never been known to boast. He doesn't play inside straights. If he tells you the thermometer registers zero you can be sure that it actually points to the 0 on the scale and not to ten above or three below—he's that kind of a man. Besides, Mr. Samuel has been feeling the Legion's pulse for several years, most of the time as department adjutant of his home State. He knows his Legion in the good old family doctor fashion.

Sometime in the month of November—several weeks before the returns of the posts which had obtained a hundred per cent membership for 1925 began to come in—Mr. Samuel, with a lack of conservatism that was highly uncharacteristic, ventured this prophecy: "We'll have 20,000 paid-up members for 1925 before New Year's Day."

Well, even as long ago as December 20th, National Headquarters had received, counted and sorted exactly 22,-457 paid-up membership cards for 1925. And at the rate the cards were coming in each day, the number of 1925 cards on New Year's Day was expected to be fully 40,-000—twice as many as Mr. Samuel's original estimate.

Well, 22,457 cards on December 20th is an over-the-top record, all right. It's the best start on a new year in the Legion's whole history. On December 20, 1923, Headquarters had received only 2,039 paid-in-advance cards on the new year, so the headstart for 1925 is exactly ten times as good as that for 1924. And this isn't the only indication that the Legion right now is heading into the greatest membership year of its history. All other signs tell the same story—the December membership duels between departments, the great and fine activity of the American Legion Auxiliary, the fire and zip of the membership drives which posts are putting on as this is written to win the Meritorious Service Citations by getting a one hundred percent membership for the new year before January 1st.

In last week's issue we mentioned Newman Millage Post of Pukwana, South Dakota, as the pace-setter for the rest of the Legion. If you read what we said then, you'll remember that this South Dakota post, in a town of 192, had already signed up 103 Legion members for 1925. That record still stands, but down in West Virginia there is at least one town with the Pukwana spirit. Greenbrier Post has its home in Ronceverte, a town with approximately 2,500 men, women and children—and the number of eligible service men in the town itself is less than a hundred. In spite of this fact Greenbrier Post rang a mighty hearty Christmas and New Year's bell by pointing to a record of exactly 318 members.

"We went out in the surrounding country and signed them up on the dotted line," writes O. C. Damewood, Past Commander of Greenbrier Post.

That's one of the reasons why the West Virginia Department has served notice that it plans to win the Henry D. Lindsley National Membership Trophy by getting the highest percentage of paid-up membership by March 1st.

Typical of the whole Legion's determination to make 1925 the Legion's biggest year is the nation-wide movement now being conducted to bring into the Legion as many as possible of the 800,000 former Navy service men in the country. Fifteen posts composed entirely of former service men of the Navy and Marine Corps started this movement at the Saint Paul National Convention by forming an association known as the Navy-Marine Posts of The American Legion. Practically every department has pledged its assistance to the association, whose first effort will be to establish a Navy-Marine Post in every city having a population of 100,000 or over. The adjutants of all departments, in conference at National Headquarters in November, adopted a resolution recommending the formation of Navy-Marine posts in each department.

The organizers of the association estimate that a very small percentage of the former service men of the Navy and Marine Corps now belong to the Legion. They point to the fact that the existing posts composed exclusively of Navy and Marine Corps service men have made exceptional records in the activities of their departments.

Credit for organizing the new association goes largely to the Minneapolis Navy-Marine Post, which was host to the other Navy and Marine posts during the Saint Paul convention. Eugene F. Galvin, Commander of the Minneapolis Post, was elected Commander of the Association. The other officers of this live-wire, go-getter organization are Wesley Masters, Mt. Gilead, Ohio, First Vice-President; John M. Dervin, Philadelphia, Pa., Second Vice-President; Fred C. Campbell, Minneapolis, Secretary and Treasurer. An advisory council consists of Charles W. Schick, of Chicago, Past Commander of the Department of Illinois; Dr. C. V. Spawr, Benton Harbor, Michigan, Past Commander of the Department of Michigan; Miss Eunice Dessez, Past Commander of Jacob Jones Post of Washington, D. C., and Herbert Stern, of Philadelphia, Past Department Vice-Commander.

From all over the country come reports of Posts mobilizing to better the 1924 record. The fight for the Lindsley Trophy is sure to be a hot one.

---

100 PERCENT MEMBERSHIP
The 1925 Goal of Every Post

First objective: As many members in 1925 as in 1924.

Second objective: Every eligible service man in town a post member.

HAS your post drawn up its plans for a membership drive which will stir up your town, arouse red-hot enthusiasm for the Legion and produce hundreds of names on the dotted line?

Is the Auxiliary unit of your post fired with the spirit of help that will make your membership drive a success?

Is the Forty and Eight lined up for the one hundred percent campaign?

Does your post know how to follow up its membership drive, so that new members will continue to come in after the fireworks of your biggest effort have been set off?

Draw up your post's member-getting battle orders now. Use the methods which have helped hundreds of Legion posts in all parts of the country enroll every eligible service man and woman in their communities. Learn how they did it by writing today for the new booklet, "Members—How to Get Them—How to Hold Them," published by the Organization and Membership Division, National Headquarters, The American Legion, Indianapolis, Indiana.

Old Paper Day comes four times a year in Brackenridge, Pennsylvania, and on each Old Paper Day members of Brackenridge Post of the Legion and squads of Boy Scout volunteers collect all the discarded newspapers and magazines which the people of the town save for them systematically every day in the year. The post sells the papers, collected on motor trucks, to a paper mill in its home town. Every Old Paper Day in Brackenridge adds $200 to Brackenridge Post's treasury. The photograph shows a Legion paper-gathering truck and a squad of the volunteer workers

A Post *That* Pays Its Way *with* Paper

EVERYBODY in Brackenridge, Pennsylvania, works for Brackenridge Post of The American Legion every day in the year—and twice as hard on Sundays. Every man and woman and almost every boy and girl is a silent partner of Brackenridge Post. And every home in the town is a link in the chain of business enterprise which Brackenridge Post has created to make its treasury grow and keep it growing. And the merchants of the town, with their widely varied stores, are important co-workers in business with the Brackenridge Legionnaires.

You will understand quickly why all this is so if you arrive in Brackenridge on a certain Saturday this winter and take note of what is going on. One of the first attention-striking things you will notice is the fact that an extraordinary number of motor trucks seem to be on the streets all through the town, each truck piled high with bundled newspapers. You discard the idea that a metropolitan newspaper is sending the fresh product of its presses out in this fashion, for the papers on the trucks are obviously old—most of them with that worn, yellowed look which papers acquire after staying for a time in cellar or attic. Then you will note that some of the trucks carry banners or signs. The banners and signs give the clew. Brackenridge Post of the Legion is making its quarterly collection of all the old newspapers and mag-

azines in the town. It is gathering up all the town's discarded reading matter which has accumulated since the last preceding collection, three months earlier.

If you're a real investigator, you'll see that the trucks coming from the streets in all sections of the town, each heavily loaded and each manned by a crew of Legionnaires and Boy Scouts, converge on the road leading toward the Allegheny River. And if you follow that road you'll come to a paper mill.

There—that's the big idea. A Legion post that collects every scrap of salable old newspapers and wastepaper in its town, hauls it to a paper mill, also in its town, and counts the cash it has made as soon as it has added up what the scales have registered during its day's work.

A mighty fine plan, of course, but it is the product of more than a bright idea and an easy-going effort. Downright hard work was necessary to make Brackenridge Post the old paper monopolist of its town, and to make the plan succeed the post had to cultivate fully the natural feeling of friendship and good will which the citizens of the town have for it.

Brackenridge had slightly fewer than 5,000 inhabitants the last time Uncle Sam counted them, and any statistician can cook up estimates of the tons of newspapers and magazines which these 5,000 read and discard in a year. Brackenridge Post wore off the points

of numerous lead pencils several years ago figuring out its possible profits and then launched its community papergathering campaign. It has been gathering paper at intervals of three months ever since that first effort. And the profits have been all that the post hoped they would be.

Each Saturday campaign brings into the post treasury approximately $200, and the post's treasury is increased usually more than $800 for each year's efforts.

The paper collections are made on Saturday because on that day most Legionnaires are able to help. A post committee handles the arrangements. For three days preceding each campaign, the town's newspapers publish conspicuous news articles which inform everybody in town that the Legionnaires will call for papers again. To simplify the collection, householders and others are asked to place their old newspapers outside their doors on the Saturday appointed. The post also has several large banners advertising the campaign which it stretches high above the principal street of the town for ten days preceding the collection.

The committee arranges for the trucks needed to make the collection—business men and factories and contractors lend them gladly. Lists are made in advance of the members of the post who can jump into working clothes on the collection Saturday, and men are *(Continued on page 13)*

EDITORIAL

FOR God and country, we associate ourselves together for the following purposes: To uphold and defend the Constitution of the United States of America; to maintain law and order; to foster and perpetuate a one hundred percent Americanism; to preserve the memories and incidents of our association in the Great War; to inculcate a sense of individual obligation to the community, state and nation; to combat the autocracy of both the classes and the masses; to make right the master of might; to promote peace and good will on earth; to safeguard and transmit to posterity the principles of justice, freedom and democracy; to consecrate and sanctify our comradeship by our devotion to mutual helpfulness.—Preamble to Constitution of The American Legion.

The Spirit of the Endowment

THE endowment campaign to raise five million dollars for the perpetuation of the Legion's child welfare and rehabilitation programs may look to some folks at first blush like nothing but a lot of hard work. Raising money, even raising a relatively modest sum of money for the relatively most important public service in the United States today, is a matter of very definite organized effort. Taken right hot off the griddle, this endowment job is just that—a job.

Once the vital appeal is realized, once the magnificent backing of all America is plainly offered, once the enormous adequacy of 11,000 aggressive American Legion posts for the task is made evident, thought turns to the deeper significance of the project.

In addition to the comforting thought of five million dollars in the bank as insurance that the care of the disabled and war orphans will never fail or falter, what does this endowment mean to the individual member of the Legion?

It means responsibility—responsibility and a high commitment to fulfill a great faith. The American people by this endowment are giving to The American Legion what it has asked for—the responsibility and privilege of caring for those who gave most to their country. Every dollar that clinks into this endowment chest is an expression of America's faith in her service sons and daughters. America, speaking through her millions of Americans, is saying, "I see it as my first and highest duty to care justly for him who suffered the scars of battle, and for the orphan child of him who fell. To this high duty I give this endowment fund. To its administration I entrust that group of Americans best fitted by experience and best proved by performance in citizenship, The American Legion."

What an investment lies in this trust, above money and above price! The Legion accepts it joyfully, grateful that the organization has made itself ready and fit for such commitment to America's weal.

"Part of Which I Was"

THE average service man's interest in his own historical record is only strong enough to let him save his cancelled bank checks, his army discharge certificate and perhaps a photograph or two of himself in uniform. But somewhere, in the bottom of a cobwebby trunk, somebody else may be saving the letters he wrote from France or from the training camps at home. For five years now fathers and mothers and wives have been obtaining fragmentary recollections of the happenings of war days, but they have never ceased complaining of the conspiracy of silence which they say still holds secret too much of what took place overseas or during tent and barrack days at home. Usually what information is imparted to the folks who waited at home is accidental or incidental, serving only to whet a curiosity which has not been dulled by the passing of five years.

The American Legion Auxiliary, however, is going to see that the records of sons and brothers and husbands are not lost to posterity, buried in the vast file rooms of the War and Navy departments. The Auxiliary, looking forward to the distant day when grandchildren will be asking questions about the war, is making the service records

of Legionnaires a part of its own membership records. Each applicant for membership in the Auxiliary copies on the reverse side of the application form she submits the Army or Navy record of the son or brother or husband whose war service gave her the privilege of joining this great society of American women. If she is entitled to membership in the Auxiliary by the service of more than one veteran—if her father, brother and husband all served, for example—she submits the service records of all.

The Auxiliary is performing a valuable service to the descendants of Legionnaires. It realizes that, unlike the Legion, it will march on through time, gaining strength and prestige with each passing year, as strong fifty years from now as today. And when the day comes when final honors have been given the last Legionnaire, the Legion's cause will still be carried forward. Today the National Heredity Committee of the Auxiliary carries on its work, a work that will be more and more appreciated as the years speed by.

What the Auxiliary is doing is especially creditable because of the fact that the five years of the Legion's history have not been sufficient to crystallize a historical background for the Legion. The Legion is so busy still making history that it does not spend much time thinking of its own past. But each year the importance of the Legion's historical efforts—nationally, in departments and in posts—is more appreciated. National Historian Eben Putnam is serving the organization well by doing everything he can to induce departments and posts to preserve all the records and documents bearing on their development and activities. Recently at a conference of all department adjutants held at National Headquarters, Mr. Putnam urged that each post hold a meeting this winter devoted to a review of the history of the post during the past five years. With the snow flying on a winter's night, what better form could a post meeting take? Winter is the season of introspection, for organizations as well as individuals. Besides, every post ought to keep its own history as faithfully as it keeps its account books. And what post wishes to bequeath to posterity merely a file of receipted bills and a roll-call?

Now That It's 1925

UNDER every joke is a basis of seriousness. Take, for example, the somewhat shopworn changes which are annually rung on the New Year's resolution and its early demise. There is something tragically pathetic as well as something funny in the picture of frail humanity aiming higher than it can hope to aspire. It has the wish, the high resolve, but it lacks the will. But the wish is something.

There are, however, resolutions which we can all make with some chance of living up to them. The obligations of American citizenship are not onerously exacting. We can all function successfully as units in the machinery of our own Government without putting ourselves to great inconvenience.

We can resolve to register, and we can register. We can vote. We can pay our poll taxes. We can pay our income taxes and see that they bear some proportionate relation to our incomes. We can serve on juries if we are invited.

Few of us in the millions-strong army of citizenship are ever asked to do more than this. None of us, in the interests of good government, ought ask to do less.

❖ ❖ ❖

Airmen at Fort Riley, Kansas, flew seven hundred miles to attend a dance. Some hop.

❖ ❖ ❖

Statisticians have not yet determined whether the quick melting prize should go to last summer's ice or this winter's coal.

A *Personal Page by* Frederick Palmer

The Things *That* Count

THERE is a question which I should like every member of Congress to put to himself daily on rising and on going to bed, until the Legion's Universal Draft Law is passed:

"What is mine and every human being's most valuable possession?"

The answer is, *life.* That is worth more to you than wealth or honors; for neither wealth nor honors can be enjoyed without life. Next in value is health. Money cannot buy that; ribbons three rows deep across your chest cannot restore it.

Lives are the great price which a nation pays in war. The sacrifice of life wins the victory and gives the penury and misery of defeat its haunting horror.

The lives of a nation's able-bodied youth are its chief capital in war—the capital of blood, flesh, bone and brain —while money is only paper and metal. Sentimentalize it and disguise it how you will war is killing and maiming the enemy until you have killed and maimed enough of him to bring him to his knees. The side which is the more skilful has to sacrifice less lives than the other. Outnumbering colleges, overwhelming intellect, high industrial organization and overflowing bank vaults are helpless and an easy victim in war unless they are walled in by the men in uniform who face death.

Those who are killed never know the welcoming plaudits of the people for the homecoming army. In the dawn of their manhood they have lost their most valuable possession.

Among the survivors are those who have lost their next most valuable possession, health. They may be minus legs, or arms, or jaws, or noses. Often maimed of mind as well as of body they hitch their way through life in a half existence. White crosses over their graves for some and disablement for others at the front! Those not in service and who have life and health never separated from their comforts and families!

YOUTH of a common country with a common stake in it! Youth, who, whatever their birth or station, have the same interest in life! Some youths going into the maw of hell while others are safe even from the flames that lick the edge of the maw! Some youths dying and being maimed in order that other youths and all the people at home and future generations may remain secure!

Does fate or do circumstances provide any more terrible inequality than this?

When war comes and the nation has to say: "I must have human sacrifice. I must send sons to death and to be maimed"—is it fair to leave the choice to volunteering or to any haphazard method?

Volunteering punishes the impulse of patriotism and rewards its absence. It is disorganized injustice, wicked, shortsighted, wasteful and inefficient. All drafts have hitherto been applied to men of fighting age for service at the front. To those drafted the nation has said:

"You do as I tell you, offer your life in the way I demand, take the pay I choose to give you, or you are no patriot and I'll punish you as a traitor."

And to all other men the nation has said:

"You I do not draft. You I do not pretend to command. For you there is no penalty of public disgrace or jail or death for disobedience. Your wife may have ten times the money that a soldier's wife has to spend. You may get as high wages as you can when labor is scarce owing to the absence of other men at the front. You may make as much money in other ways as you can. I entreat you to keep busy making bullets for the men at the front. Won't you, please? If you will, you will be the real hero"—and *not* the man at the front.

A hundred years hence this injustice may be considered as brutal and out of date as hanging men for thievery or burning witches is today.

As one of the readers of this page, L. B. Harnish, puts it in a letter to me:

"If the government can compel one man to stop bullets with his body, and the government has that right, then it should also compel the other man to make bullets with his hands."

The justice of equality and of true democracy will say in the next war:

"Every man and woman will be drafted to obey orders for government-fixed pay. Each shall do the part for which he is fitted."

THE man whose capital is money or brain shall be forced to give the service of that capital for the same pay as the man whose capital is the body he exposes to fire. The man at home will still have the advantage in that he is sure of retaining his greatest asset, which is life, while the man at the front may lose his.

With all manhood, all energy drafted, then those who are drafted into civilian labor would not be demobilized from war pay until the returning soldiers could take up civil life again under something like even conditions. Thus the people behind the lines might feel in small measure what the soldier himself knows in cruel measure, that war is hell, and they will accordingly take more interest in keeping the country out of war.

This would ensure the end of the bitterness which returning soldiers have justifiably felt. The just and natural demand for pensions would not be heard. For the first time in the history of wars all our thought, after the war, would be centered on adequate compensation for mothers and wives who had lost their breadwinners, and on the care of the disabled. There would be an end of profiteering and of the glory stuff during the war and of neglect of war victims after the war.

Governments provide buildings, public works and schools for future generations. Individuals buy homes and save money for the future. They plant seed for next year's harvest. They insure against fire and disaster. At every turn we have the teaching of that prevision which makes the difference between the short sight of the savage and the long sight of civilization.

Yet we do not insure against the greatest of all disasters, against the day when war comes. We make no provision that the injustice of the past shall not be repeated when the next generation is called to the sacrifice.

The Legion's proposed Universal Draft Law makes this provision. This law is written out of bloody and costly experience as the Legion's great contribution to the future. Is there any Legionnaire, or wife or mother of a Legionnaire, who does not hold that it is our duty to see that law passed in order to save us from the errors of the half-draft of the World War?

On Agin, Off Agin

By Wallgren

The American Legion: Sponsor
of International Good Will

Ten guesses as to where this picture was taken. You're all wrong—it shows Boy Scouts of the Legion-guided troop of Tampico, Mexico, enjoying an outing in their home town. Most of the youngsters are related to members of the post, but those that aren't get the same grounding in the American spirit

How many Legionnaires ever give a thought to the fact that the Legion has posts in foreign countries which fill, for the ex-service men abroad, a need perhaps even greater than that of the veterans here at home? And in a foreign city, even more than is likely in New York or North Dakota or New Mexico, the Americans look to a well-run Legion post as the leader in national and patriotic activities.

Tampico Post of the Department of Mexico is the largest post in the Legion outside the territorial limits of the United States. Here are 375 members of one post from the perhaps 5,000 American residents in this Mexican city of 100,000.

To keep the Americans American, and to keep their children American, is a real task for the Legion in a foreign country. How is it to be accomplished? For the American there is surrounded with the influence of the country he lives in. American customs, American traditions, American ideas tend to fade out of his life unless he gets back to this country occasionally.

In Tampico, for example, July 4th was the only American holiday observed by Americans until three years ago. Memorial Day and Armistice Day were wholly out of the picture.

The Legion post took hold of the situation. On Memorial Day the post now holds services in its club room. Church services are held on Armistice Day, and a big dinner is given on Armistice Eve. The Americans are now reminded of

Some of these all-American youngsters have never set eyes or foot on the United States, but Tampico Post of the Legion helps to keep alive in them the spirit of their American heritage

their patriotic holidays, and are consequently brought that much more frequently to contemplate with some seriousness the responsibilities and privileges of their citizenship.

But the Americanism of Tampico Post is never of the sort which can be in any sense objectionable to Mexicans. It is all aimed at the goal of a better understanding between the people of the two countries. And it is helping to give the Mexicans a comprehension of some of the ideals of America.

To most Americans who have never been in Mexico the typical Mexican is thought of as the Mexican who works on our railroad rights of way—a somewhat undersized, not particularly clean or particularly intelligent individual who could under no circumstances be admissible to the society of any average American community. And the movies have helped along this idea, for a few years back no thriller was complete without a Mexican villain who done the hero dirt and tried to abduct the beautiful heero-yne.

The American who harbors this conception of a Mexican would be quite astonished to know that the Mexican of about his own place in the world considers that all Americans are a loud-mouthed, ill-mannered crowd of boors, who drink too much whenever they get the chance, and fairly thirst for the chance to do murder. Yet, without exaggeration, this is the idea which the Mexican public has of Americans.

Of course our own ideas of the Mexicans are as far wrong as are their

(Continued on page 16)

Make BIG MONEY!
—IN RADIO—
We Need Men—Can You Qualify?

Ozarka representatives make real money because they give real values and deliver a real service. For instance, there is a 4-tube Ozarka Instrument for loud speaker operation, giving wide range of reception at $39.50. Our men demonstrate Ozarka Instruments and Install. The Instrument makes the sale easy by its performance. We train you to know radio and our methods, make you worthy to wear the Ozarka button as our accredited representative. Previous experience is not necessary. In fact we prefer to do our own educating. If you have a clean record, are industrious, and have saved up a little cash, here's a real opportunity, if you can qualify for an exclusive territory. We already have 2247 representatives. Territory going fast.

FREE, LARGE Illustrated BOOK

WRITE Today for Illustrated book No. 101 that gives the entire Ozarka Plan. Don't fail to give the name of your county.

OZARKA, Inc.
859 Washington Blvd.
CHICAGO

4 Tube Sets As Low as $39.50

EARN MONEY AT HOME

YOU can earn $1 to $2 an hour in your spare time writing show cards. No canvassing or soliciting. We instruct you by our new simple Directograph System, supply you with work and pay you cash each week. Write today for full particulars and free booklet.

WEST-ANGUS SHOW CARD SERVICE LIMITED
Authorized Capital $1,250,000.00
180 Colborne Building,   Toronto, Can.

WANT WORK AT HOME?

Earn $18 to $60 a week retouching photos. Men or women. No selling or canvassing. We teach you, guarantee employment and furnish working outfit free. Limited offer. Write today.

ARTCRAFT STUDIOS, Dept. 1, 3908 Sheridan Rd., Chicago

$3 Brings you a Genuine UNDERWOOD
TYPEWRITER

10 DAYS FREE TRIAL Your $3.00 unconditionally returned if at end of 10 days you are not satisfied with this late model UNDERWOOD typewriter rebuilt by the famous Shipman Ward process.

GREAT PRICE SAVING Direct to you from the factory to the world by our money saving methods.

EASY MONTHLY PAYMENTS So small that you will not notice it while you enjoy the use of this wonderful machine.

FREE BOOK OF FACTS Explaining Shipman Ward's wonderful system of rebuilding typewriters and also valuable information about the typewriter industry both instructive and entertaining.

Act Today! Mail Coupon

5 Year Guarantee

Shipman Ward Mfg. Company
2511 Shipman Building
Montrose & Ravenswood
Aves., Chicago

Please mail me a copy of your free book of facts explaining bargain offer.

Name..
St. and No..................................
City.........................State.............

He Skipped *from* Sailor Knots *to* Legal Tangles

JUST because Warren L. Shobert wanted to be a lawyer—he had always wanted to be a lawyer—it seemed as though fate was against him. It the first place it looked as though he would have to settle down into the harness of the family business, monuments, back at Bloomsburg, Pennsylvania. And Shobert didn't want to do it. He didn't like the monument business, and, anyhow—he wanted to be a lawyer.

While he was figuring out ways and means to get to law school—and sometimes he thought he just about had a way worked out to make it—the United States went into the war. So Shobert, with that almost universal combination of a desire to serve his country and a reluctance to give up his life's ambition, joined up.

He joined the navy. Eventually he became a Chief Pharmacists' Mate, and during most of the war he served on the U. S. S. *Florida*, operating in the North Sea with the British Grand Fleet. What the North Sea operations were like is history—not particularly pleasant history for the men who were engaged there. For while the operations were highly successful, the duty was about as cold, and wet, and generally uncomfortable as was the common lot of men in active service. Many a strong man's health broke under the strain of it. Shobert was one of the casualties. He was taken ill, and at the end of the war transferred to Fort Lyons, Colorado, for medical treatment.

Finally Shobert was discharged at Fort Lyons, with a medical survey. And he didn't know just what to do. "My strength and physical disability would not permit me to go back home," he explains. "It was a question which way to turn. Then came the offer of rehabilitation from the Government."

Shobert made good at the University; he made very good. He graduated in three years, after taking full part in the activities of the university outside the class-room as well as inside. He belonged to a social fraternity; was president of an honorary

law fraternity;; commander of The American Legion Post; a member of the Boosters' Club; and president of the Combined Laws.

Now all of this time Shobert was not strong. But the climate, and the joy of life now that he was actually on the way to becoming a lawyer, were healing his disability. If the training pay had been insufficient to meet living expenses, and if Shobert had had to try to work part of his way in his outside hours, it is a question whether he could have come through school in as good condition as when he entered. As it was, he ascribes his steady improvement in health to the care he was able to take of himself. "We could devote our entire efforts and time to our studies and the care of our health," is the way he describes it.

But even with his diploma earned in three school years, Shobert was entitled to another year of study. He took it in the law school of the University of Utah, in which State he intended to practice. So, to his 1922 Colorado diploma he added a Utah sheepskin dated 1923.

Promptly after his graduation from Utah and his admission to the bar, he and another vocational trainee, R. Leslie Hedrick, began practicing law at Salt Lake City. The climate was suitable; and the local courts dealt with the types of cases which they had specialized on in college.

The firm of Shobert and Hedrick has a suite of offices in one of Salt Lake City's good office buildings. "Successful?" does someone ask. "What? A pair of young lawyers only a year out of law school, and *successful*? Who ever heard of such a thing?"

But the fact remains that they have been successful. During the first year's practice, Shobert and Hedrick handled approximately 350 suits in the various counties of Utah.

And certain it is that the United States Navy overlooked a good bet when it was recruiting young men in the early days of the war. It might have stimulated enlistments materially by advertising the slogan:

"Join the Navy and Learn the Law!"

Warren Shobert's health went to smash in Navy service, but by hard work he got to be a lawyer, and he's making good

only $14.35

MIRACO RADIO GETS 'EM COAST to COAST

FOR THIS GUARANTEED LONG DISTANCE RADIO

Users everywhere report Miraco Tuned Radio Frequency receivers pick up programs coast to coast; outperform sets three times as costly. Send for proof they are radio's most amazing values in powerful long distance sets. One tube guaranteed, completely assembled outfit, as illustrated, list $14.35. Three tube guaranteed loud speaker outfit, list $29.50.

SEND POSTAL TODAY
for latest bulletins and special offer. It will interest you.
MIDWEST RADIO CORP'N
Pioneer Builders of Sets
464-H, E. 6th St., Cincinnati, O.

HOTELS WANT MEN AND WOMEN

FOR POSITIONS PAYING $150 TO $500 MONTHLY

80,000 trained hotel employees wanted this year. We train you and help you secure position—good pay to start and rapid advancement to executive positions for earnest, able workers. Prepare at home, spare time; cost moderate, terms easy. Write for free booklet H-152.
STANDARD BUSINESS TRAINING INST.,
Buffalo, N. Y.

FREE

$20 Fine Tone Musical Instruments

We have a wonderful new copyrighted system of teaching note music by mail. To first pupils in each locality we will give free a $20 superb Violin, Tenor Banjo, Ukulele, Hawaiian Guitar, Banjo, Mandolin, Banjo-Ukulele, Banjo-Mandolin, Cornet or Banjo-Guitar absolutely free. Also teach Piano and Organ. Very small charge for lessons only. Four lessons will teach you several pieces. Over 100,000 successful players. We guarantee success or no charge. Complete outfit free. Write today, Dept 166. No obligation.
Slingerland School of Music, 1815 Orchard St., Chicago, Ill.

YOU CAN OIL PAINT

Amazing new method teaches men or women to earn after first lesson. OIL PAINT photos at home—portraits, landscapes or art subjects. Earn $18 to $100 and more a week. FREE OIL PAINT OUTFIT. Graduates furnished employment. Send now for free illustrated book.
PICTORIAL ART STUDIOS, Inc.
Department A-23   2731 No. Clark St., Chicago

PATENTS

Write for my free Guide Books "How to Obtain a Patent" and "Invention and Industry" and "Record of Invention" blank before disclosing inventions. Send model or sketch of your invention for instructions. Promptness assured. No charge for above information. Clarence A. O'Brien, Registered Patent Lawyer, 1925 Security Bank Building, directly across street from Patent Office, Washington, D. C.—Adv.

AGENTS SELL PANTS

At Lower Prices Than Ready Made Pants
Big Money Making Proposition
FREE SALESMAN OUTFIT
Showing 200 different patterns. No selling experience required. Commissions paid in advance. Write today. Give references. Outfit sent immediately. No deposit required.
Washington Square Tailoring Co., Inc., Dept. 29
832 Broadway   New York City

13 WEEKS FOR 15 CENTS

The Pathfinder

You've heard your neighbor praise this wonderful weekly magazine that 3 million people read. Unbiased digest of national or world affairs. Check full of just the kind of reading you want. Science, politics, travel, fun, fashions, question box, books, health—entertainment and instruction for all. Send 15c (coin or stamps) today for this big paper on trial 13 weeks or $1 for 1 year (52 issues).
PATHFINDER, 502 Langdon Sta., Washington, D. C.

WONDERFUL POULTRY BOOK

The Nation's Great Poultry Manual, 144 Pages. Beautiful Pictures. All about Mrs. Berry's success with Pure-Bred Poultry and Hatchery; also short cuts to profits. Feeding, Housing, Culling, Disease and Remedy information. Makes LOW PRICES on Pure-Quality Fowls, Eggs, Chicks, Brooders, Supplies, Etc. Send only 5c to help mail.
BERRY'S POULTRY FARM Box 52 CLARINDA, IOWA

A Post That Pays Its Way with Paper

(Continued from page 7)

assigned to each truck. Boy Scout volunteers are also listed and assigned to the trucks. Each worker is notified in advance of the starting place of the truck on which he will work. With the list of all the trucks posted in advance, rivalry to make the largest collections makes the campaign a sporting event.

As fast as each truck picks up a load, it is driven to the paper mill. The mill gives each truck commander a weight slip showing the number of pounds of paper on each load delivered. At the end of the day these slips are delivered by truck leaders to the post committee.

Brackenridge Post officials say their whole plan is dependent upon the habit of saving old papers. The citizens of Brackenridge were quick to appreciate the possibilities of giving real help to the post at a slight expenditure of effort, and so, today, everybody in Brackenridge saves newspapers systematically. Morning newspapers are not thrown into waste-paper receptacles by men on their way to work, but are saved through the day and carried home in the evening to be added to the family's accumulation. And the bulky Sunday newspapers no longer are cast into the furnace simply to get them out of the way.

Yes — everybody in Brackenridge works with and for Brackenridge Post of the Legion.

TAPS

The deaths of Legion members are chronicled in this column. In order that it may be complete, post commanders are asked to designate an official or member to notify the Weekly of all deaths. Please give name, age, military record.

FRANK E. CROWLEY, *Commonwealth Edison Post, Chicago, Ill.* D. Nov. 7.

JOSEPH F. MARTIN, *Henry Sullins Post, Vienna, Ill.* D. Dec. 10, aged 32. Served with Co. H, 58th Inf.

WILLIAM J. MORRISEY, *Archie Wood Post, Clarksville, Tenn.* D. Nov. 26, aged 33. Served with Infantry.

HERBERT L. RICKS, *Bernard Gill Post, Shawnee, Okla.* D. Nov. 25, aged 29. Served with Co. D, 320th M. G. Bn., 82d Div.

EDWARD G. SHERLOCK, *Michael J. Perkins Post, South Boston, Mass.* D. Dec. 11, aged 68. Lt. Com. U. S. N.

GEORGE SPANOS, *George Dilboy Post, New York City.* D. Dec. 18, aged 32. Served with Co. K, First Pioneer Inf.

BROOKS M. THORNE, *Candler County Post, Metter, Ga.* D. Dec. 14. Served with 6th Co., 157th Depot Brigade.

JOHN M. TRIMBLE, *Lancaster (Pa.) Post.* D. at U. S. Veterans Bureau Hospital No. 68, Beacon, N. Y., Dec. 16. Served with 316th Inf.

CARL J. WALDMAN, *Charles J. Wagner Post, Leipsic, O.* D. Dec. 12, aged 29. Served with Co. I, 329th Inf. 83d Div.

HARVEY A. WILLIAMS, *Lancaster (Pa.) Post.* D. Dec. 16. Served with Co. B, 103d Supply Tr.

RICHARD A. YOUNG, JR., *L. B. Faulk Post, Monroe, La.* D. Dec. 5, aged 38. Major 156th Inf.

ALL editorial and general communications to this publication should be addressed to The American Legion Weekly, Indianapolis, Indiana, where the Legion's official magazine is now printed. Advertising correspondence should be addressed either to the Eastern Advertising Office of the Weekly, 331 Madison Avenue, New York City, or the Western Advertising Office, 22 West Monroe Street, Chicago.

DIAMONDS·WATCHES
Sent for inspection without one penny down

LADY JANE $37.50
QUEEN MARY $75.00

No security required; no red tape; we trust you absolutely. Examine diamond at your leisure—wear it 30 days FREE. Send it back at our expense if not entirely satisfactory. You are not out a penny. Do not wait longer—a few cents a day will make you the owner of a sparkling, perfectly cut, blue-white diamond, set in 18 Karat Purity White Gold.

New Low Prices and Terms None Can Beat

Why pay full price? Examine our diamonds. It costs nothing to see diamonds. After being thoroly satisfied it's the largest value for your money you ever saw, keep the ring and pay balance in small monthly payments.
Wear 30 Days FREE

Solid Gold Case Illinois Mvt.   **Ladies' New Elite Wrist Watch**

This artistic, dependable Ladies' Wrist Watch fitted with genuine Illinois Springfield movements. A perfect timepiece. Beautiful 14 Karat white or green solid gold cases. Ask for New Watch Book showing cases in all the new shapes and designs. Watch sent on approval and sold on payments. $3.50 a month.

FREE Watch and Diamond catalog sent post-paid. Send for yours today.

WEDDING RINGS
Beautiful hand engraved Purity White Gold Wedding Ring to match diamond rings.
$2.00 a Month

Santa Fe Watch Co.
Sole Distributor of the Santa Fe Special Watch

SANTA FE WATCH COMPANY,
183 Thomas Building, Topeka, Kan.
Please send prepaid and without obligation your Watch and Diamond Book Free, explaining your "No Money Down" Offer on Watches and Diamonds

Name.....................................
Address...................................
State.....................................

MATCH

A new pair of trousers will give an extra year's wear to that suit. Send sample of material or the vest and we will match with new trousers. If we can't suit you, will return vest prepaid. This is a chance for real economy—send the vest now. Satisfaction guaranteed.

Superior Match Pants Co.
Dept V, 115 S. Dearborn Street
Chicago, Ill.

MAKE MONEY SELL MADISON SHIRTS

Direct from our factory to wearer. Easily sold. Over one million satisfied wearers. No capital or experience required. Large steady income. Many earn $100 to $150, weekly. Territory now being allotted. Write For Free Samples.
MADISON SHIRT MILL, 564 B'way, New York

Easy to Play
Easy to Pay

BUESCHER
True-Tone
Saxophone

BENNIE KRUEGER
Director Bennie
Krueger and His
Orchestra, Bruns-
wick Records.

Easiest of all instruments to
play and one of the most
beautiful. Three first lessons
sent free give you a quick
easy start—in a few weeks
you can be playing popular
tunes. No teacher neces-
sary. You can take your
place in a band or orchestra
in ninety days, if you so desire.
Most popular instrument for dance
orchestras, home entertainments,
church, lodge and school. A Saxophone player is always popular
socially and has many opportunities to
earn money. Six Days' Trial and easy
payments arranged.　　　(106)

Free Saxophone Book Shows all
models and gives first lesson chart; also pictures of famous
professionals and orchestras. Just send your name for a copy.
Mention any other instrument in which you may be interested.

BUESCHER BAND INSTRUMENT CO.
Everything in Band and Orchestra Instruments
442 BUESCHER BLOCK - - ELKHART, INDIANA

They Beat the Forty-Niners by Four Thousand Years

(Continued from page 5)

California citizens and motor tourists. Visalia Post proudly recalls the day last summer when it first paid homage to the tree that is the oldest and largest living thing in the world. On that day, in the presence of hundreds of Legionnaires who had traveled sixty miles, most of the way over high mountain roads, it initiated into the Legion the superintendent of Sequoia National Park, Colonel John R. White. An improvised meeting hall was placed at the foot of the biggest tree, and the Commander's table, the corner posts and seats were all covered with redwood bark. Besides the Legionnaires a thousand persons looked down from the mountainside while the Legion's full initiatory ceremonial was carried out. A baseball game and a varied entertainment program followed the initiation, and an enormous campfire was held in the evening. So impressive was the whole affair that the plan to make the outing an annual event was immediately decided on.

And now, while the winter snows fly in the Sierras, the Legion in another section of the State, in San Mateo County, on the peninsula across San Francisco Bay from the city of San Francisco, is putting the final beautifying touches on an American Legion Memorial Park of 314 acres. Members of the San Mateo County Council of The American Legion are the park commissioners for the redwood preserve which was purchased with public funds but improved by working parties of Legionnaires.

Make Money Wearing This FREE CAP
Just Wear This Beautiful Hand-
Tailored FREE Cap and Make
Big Money in Your Spare Time!

I want to give you a FREE Cap. I know your
friends will be delighted with its class, style
and fit and you will make a generous profit
taking their orders. These caps are genuine
hand tailored, made to individual measure. Nine out of
ten men will order right away. Big profit on every sale.

$10 A DAY EASY FOR YOU
Send Name Quick—No Money
McDonald made $68 in one week. Hampton made $7.65 in four hours.
Schmidt increased his salary from $35 a week to almost $75! And you
can do every bit as well. Send your name right away and I'll tell you
how to make $10 a day, also secure a Taylor Cap for your use. Write at
once. J. W. Taylor, Pres., Taylor Cap Mfrs., Dept 13-A Cincinnati, Ohio.

Save $38.80
Take advantage of the great saving we offer
on the genuine, world-famous, ball-bearing,
long-wearing L. C. Smith Typewriter. Late
model machines, standard size, up-to-date in
every way, at remarkably low prices.

TEN DAYS' FREE TRIAL
Test it thoroughly—no obligation.

SEND NO MONEY A YEAR TO PAY Low Prices
Easy Terms
Guaranteed Five Years
We do the most perfect and highest at a job of rebuilding known to
the typewriter industry. Our machines do perfect work and last for
years and years. And like new. The L. C. Smith is the easiest machine
to operate and you can easily type your own letters. Complete lessons
on typewriting, also our 5 Year Guarantee with every machine.

FREE—Send today for Free Booklet of Valuable Typewriter
Information, Big Catalog and our Special Offer.

SMITH TYPEWRITER SALES CO.
400-360 E East Grand Avenue　　Chicago, Illinois

Make **$75.00** a Week and up, selling
our fine made-to-measure, all-wool
suits, direct to wearer. Biggest values—
positively sell on sight. Biggest commissions paid in advance. We attend to de-
livery and collections. 6x9 swatch samples—over 100 styles all one price—furnished
FREE. Part or full time men write at once.

W. Z. Gibson, Inc., 161 W. Harrison St., Dept. A-405, Chicago

BECOME AN EXPERT
ACCOUNTANT

Executive Accountants command big salaries. Thousands of firms
need them. Only 9,000 Certified Public Accountants in U. S. Many
are earning $3,000 to $10,000 a year. We train you thoroughly in your
spare time for C. P. A. examinations or executive accounting positions. Knowledge of bookkeeping unnecessary to begin. Our course is
under the personal supervision of William B. Castenholz, A. M.,
C. P. A., former Comptroller and Instructor, University of Illinois;
also former Director of the Illinois Society of C. P. A.'s; and of the
National Association of Cost Accountants. He is assisted by a large
staff of C. P. A.'s, including members of the American Institute of
Accountants. Low tuition fee—easy terms. Write now for information.

LaSalle Extension University, Dept. 1361-H Chicago
The Largest Business Training Institution in the World

It's a Shame to Take the Money

(Continued from page 4)

on this year's play. The ex-waiter didn't win his business. He built it up between 1917 and 1922, during a time that he never made a bet on a horse race.

The town I refer to supports four or five hand books—agents of big bookmakers in other cities. The chief of these told me that one-third of his customers were women. Every week-day morning he makes the rounds, paying off those who had winners the previous day and taking wagers on horses entered on the current day's cards. He has been making book in this town twenty years!

At Cincinnati I talked with the editor and publisher of one of the most successful racing papers in the United States. His business is proof that the racing paper that gives the most information and picks the most winners is the paper that the racing public will support. Seven years ago this editor was a sort of carpet-bag publisher. He went from one city to another where race meetings were being held, carrying his printing plant with him in boxes. He was getting out a little pink sheet containing past performances and "selections for today." I recall the first copy of it I ever saw. It was at the entrance to the fair grounds at New Orleans. I had been there playing the races without much success, so when I picked up this little pink sheet at the entrance to the park I decided I'd follow the paper's selections that day. The paper's handicapper picked five winners and those five winners got me out of the barrel, as the saying goes. Later I met the pink sheet's handicapper. It was the editor's wife, the greatest handicapper of race horses I've met in the nine years I've been around race tracks.

The wife gave the players winners while the husband gave them such high-class technical information about past performances of horses in training that the racing public began to sit up and take notice. In seven years that little pink sheet has grown until today it is installed in a permanent home at Cincinnati and is valued at $250,000.

Further evidence that the betting public will rally to the support of anybody that can give it real information is furnished by the experience another expert dopester had with a little sheet in New York. This paper made its first appearance on Broadway in 1921. It was called the "green sheet" by the players—"that damn green rag" by the players, or bookmakers. It picked winners—five and sometimes six on a six-race card. Broadway welcomed it with whoops of joy. There was always a wild scramble to buy the green sheet when it got on the street. Men literally fought for it. I've seen policemen who tried to protect newsboys who sold the papers have their uniforms literally torn from their backs in the mad scramble of purchasers. The regular price of the paper was ten cents. Race followers offered a dollar.

The green sheet's handicapper had a phenomenal run of luck that season. Broadway followed his selections and Broadway cashed more bets than it had ever cashed before. Chorus girls, waiters, bartenders, policemen, firemen—everybody became big winners. Handbook after handbook along the Great White Way bit the dust like redskins in a Cooper novel.

By giving winners the owner of the green sheet took a shoe string and ran it into a shoe factory. Bookmakers tried to buy him out, but the paper wasn't for sale. The public—that is, the speculatively inclined public—made it the most valuable racing paper in the East. Service got 'em.

But, despite all the information available through racing journals, professional handicappers' selections, cartoontipsters, and information sent out by owners, trainers and jockeys, the bettor has only one chance in fifty of winning, according to my friend the bookmaker. Only a very small percentage beat the races, while a great many lose most of their earnings year after year. In the history of the American turf the number who have made fortunes in the betting ring can be counted on your fingers, while the players who have lost their all are as numerous as the stars.

Post Adjutants!

Get Your Ideas Over With a Bang!—Listen!!!

You can't listen unless you have ears—you can't read unless it's PRINTED!

We, of the Legion, know the value of the printed word and here in Indianapolis is THE POST PRINTING SERVICE, prompt, efficient and reasonable, is at the call of every post that has a printing problem.

Cuts illustrate your story—the one at the head of this column only costs a Dollar —and, as the Chinese say, "A picture is worth a Thousand words"—you can say a lot with a few of these. We've got 60 others, all different, at the same price; discounts on orders over 5.

Post Pep Postals drag delinquent members to Post Meetings, Parades, Anniversaries, Dinners and Social Affairs, without causing any kick—au contraire they have the effect of bringing in the Wandering Sheep with wide grins—these Pep cards are funny—Get some! Every other Printing Need is our job—Ideas, Cartoons, Drawings, Layouts, Multigraphing, Halftones and Electros are among the multiplicity of printing requirements handled here.

Hundreds of Legion Posts know our Service, hundreds have still to know us and what we can do to solve their Printing Puzzles.

IF IT CAN BE PRINTED—WE DO IT!
POST PRINTING SERVICE
Dept. H
American Legion Weekly, Indianapolis, Ind.

BIG VALUE for 10 Cts.

6 Songs, words and music; 25 Pictures Pretty Girls; 40 Ways to Make Money; 1 Joke Book; 1 Book on Love; 1 Magic Book; 1 Book Letter Writing; 1 Dream Book and Fortune Teller; 1 Cook Book; 1 Base Ball Book, gives rules for games; 1 Toy Maker Book; Language of Flowers; 1 Morse Telegraph Alphabet; 12 Chemical Experiments; Magic Age Table; Great North Pole Game; 100 Conundrums; 3 Puzzles; 12 Games; 30 Verses for Autograph Albums. All the above by mail for 10 cts. and 2 cts. postage.
ROYAL SALES CO., Desk 863   Norwalk, Conn.

MAKE MONEY AT HOME

YOU can earn money at home in your spare time making show cards. No canvassing or soliciting. We show you how, supply you work at home no matter where you live and pay you cash for all work done. Full particulars and booklet free. Write today.
AMERICAN SHOW CARD SYSTEM LIMITED
179 Adams Building   Toronto, Canada

$23.50 THINK of an all-wool, tailored-to-measure Suit or Topcoat for only $23.50! That's what *you can sell* every man in your town this Spring. Make $75 a week—and up—*right from the start!* Write us today.
THE STYLE-CENTER TAILORING CO., Dept. G, Cincinnati, O.

Learn to Mount Birds

Learn at home to mount birds, animals, game heads; tan furs, make rugs and robes. Complete lessons. Easily and quickly learned by men, boys and women.
FREE Be a **Taxidermy** Book. Tells all about it. Every sportsman, trapper and Nature lover should know this wonderful, fascinating art. Save your trophies. Big profits. Success guaranteed. 75,000 graduates. Investigate. Write for Free Book.
Northwestern School of Taxidermy 2251 Elwood Bldg., Omaha, Neb.

OUTFIT REUNIONS

Announcements for this column must be received three weeks in advance of the events with which they are concerned.

33D DIV. HEADQUARTERS CLUB—Reunion at Hotel Sherman, Chicago, Ill., Jan. 23, at 8 p. m. Maj. Gen. George Bell, Jr., guest of honor. Address Frank A. Biederman, secretary-treasurer, 1922 W. Lake St., Chicago. Phone Seeley 8375.

35TH DIV.—Former members send names, old organization and present mailing address to the Secretary, Ray Hockett, office of State Highway Engineer, Topeka, Kan., or to Thomas O. Bourke, 1104 Union Ave., Kansas City, Mo.

PATRIOTIC QUIZ NO. 3

1. What American commander-in-chief wore the uniform of a private in his army when he accepted the surrender of an enemy general?

2. What American poet was forced to resign a government position because his writings were regarded as obscene?

3. What is the largest State east of the Mississippi River?

4. What armed conflict did the United States wage without making a formal declaration of war or signing a treaty of peace?

5. What President was criticized for going fishing on Memorial Day?

Answers next week.

ANSWERS TO LAST WEEK'S QUIZ

1. Robert E. Lee, superintendent of the United States Military Academy at West Point from 1852 to 1855 and commander-in-chief of the Confederate forces in the Civil War, became president of Washington and Lee University, Lexington, Virginia, shortly after the war and served until his death in 1870.

2. The purchase of Alaska from Russia for $7,200,000 in 1867 through a treaty negotiated by William H. Seward, Secretary of State, was characterized at the time as "Seward's Folly."

3. The highest percentage of casualties ever sustained by American troops was in the Battle of Little Big Horn, in what is now the State of Montana, on June 25, 1876, when General George A. Custer and a detachment consisting of a third of the Seventh United States Cavalry (265 in all) were wiped out by the Sioux Indians. Curley, a half-breed scout accompanying Custer, was the only survivor.

4. The Russo-Japanese War of 1904 was formally ended by the Treaty of Portsmouth, signed in the New Hampshire city. It was on the initiative of President Roosevelt that the two nations conducted the negotiations.

5. Horace Greeley, candidate for President on the Democratic and Independent Republican tickets in 1872, died on November 29th of that year, twenty-four days after his defeat at the polls.

Play It on a Hohner

Everybody likes good music. Nearly everybody would like to play a musical instrument. And very soon everybody *will* be playing one, for *anybody* can play a Hohner Harmonica.

Twelve million music lovers, young and old, have learned to call the Hohner Harmonica "That Musical Pal of Mine." They know that there's nothing like good music for happiness, and nothing like a Hohner for good music.

Don't hum—play it on a Hohner. Get one today—50¢ up—and ask for the Free Instruction Book. If your dealer is out of copies, write M. Hohner, Inc., Dept. 163, New York City.

If you want a musical treat ask to hear Victor Record 19421, by Borrah Minevitch.

200 Sheets—100 Envelopes

$1.00 Postage Prepaid

High grade, clear, white bond paper. Unusually smooth writing surface. Size 6 x 7 inches with envelopes to match. Has that crisp, crackly "feel" that identifies it to everyone as superior quality stationery. Special handy box keeps paper and envelopes in order and easily reached, preventing waste.

Your Name and Address Printed FREE! on every sheet and envelope, in rich dark blue, up to 4 lines. Type is Plate Gothic, designed especially for clearness and good taste. Makes a personal stationery you will be delighted to use. An ideal gift printed with your friend's name. This stationery, unprinted, would ordinarily cost you more than $1.50; our large production so narrow margin makes this special offer possible.

Just send your name and address (write or print clearly) with $1.00 (West of Denver and outside the U. S. $1.10) and this generous box of stationery will come to you neatly packed, postage prepaid. Money returned if you are not more than satisfied. Order today!
National Stationery Co. 2251 Lincoln Highway, Batavia, Illinois

Anyone CAN LEARN!

No talent or experience necessary. Fascinating work. Pays big money. Complete instruction book TELLS ABOUT Alphabets, Colors, HOW TO MIX PAINTS, Show Cards, Window Board and Wall Signs, Ready-made Letters, Gilding, Tricks of the TRADE, etc. Gives 100 Alphabets and Designs. Book bound in flexible imit. leather, gold edges, and four-ball bearing Show Card Pens, Box, Oil, etc., all postpaid. Form 1. Box. No. O. D. 10c extra. OgilviePub. Co., 57 Rose St., Dept. 47, New York

EARN MONEY *IMMEDIATELY*—WE FURNISH EQUIPMENT TO START

FREE *a wonderful* Book on Finger Prints

Full of thrilling crime mysteries solved through finger print evidence by America's greatest experts. Gripping illustrations. True stories. You can learn the Finger profession at home in spare time. Write today. Get full details.
Special Offer Big surprise in store for you. Book and offer free. Write now.
UNIVERSITY OF APPLIED SCIENCE
1920 Sunnyside Avenue, Dept. 40-81   Chicago, Ill.

Dont Hum

WANTED!
Man with Car

To Run Store On Wheels

Sell the largest, finest quality line of daily necessities from your car. No experience necessary. Hundreds now making

$200 TO $500 A MONTH

Our proposition is entirely different from all others. Our advertising half sells the goods for you. Premiums, samples and gifts all make business come your way. Business is permanent, pleasant and profitable.

BE A DOUBLE MONEY MAKER

Two entirely different lines, 241 items, a sale at every home. Two lines mean two profits. We will give you liberal credit. Write for details about our new proposition.
FURST-McNESS CO., Dept. 20 Freeport, Ill.

NEW KIND OF TIRE!
Amazing new invention—goes right into your present tire—gives you a new kind of tire. Prevents punctures, rim cuts, blow-outs, and delivers 20,000 to 30,000 miles from ordinary cords. Makes high pressure tires ride like balloons.

AGENTS THINK what you can earn with a device that makes ordinary cords deliver.. **20,000 MILES**

Agents and salesmen cleaning up. Richardson earned $57.20 in one day. Cobb sold $17,000 in first year. Every car owner or fleet owner a prospect. Liberal commission. Full cooperation from big, old established company. Write quick for exclusive territory offer and full details.
COFFIELD TIRE PROTECTOR CO., 1801 Court St., Dayton, O.

140 Egg Incubator $13.25 30 Days Trial

Freight Paid east of Rockies. Hot water copper tanks, double walls, dead air space. Made of Redwood. double glass doors, all set up complete, ready to use. With Brooder, $17.75—180-Egg Incubator $15.75, with Brooder, $22.50. Send for FREE Catalog TODAY or order direct.
Wisconsin Incubator Co., Box 136, Racine, Wis.

Sell $23.50 ALL WOOL Suits Earn $10,000 a Year

Hustlers earn $3,000 to $10,000 a year, depending on territory and industry. Our suits are all pure wool, union made, with hand tailoring. Topcoats have genuine satin lining. Money back guarantee. Protected territory and liberal commission in advance. Experience helpful. Prefer men over 35. This is a rare opportunity for an honest, energetic man to get into a big paying business with large, well established house. Apply W Harvey, Box 66, Chicago

$20 A DAY EASY

That's the average of our men selling elegant, individual, distinctive, tailored shirts. Exclusive patterns. "BUILT ON HONOR TO HONOR THEIR MAKER!" Direct from our large, airy mills to wearer. Out of ordinary values. Tremendous demand. Big repeat business. We deliver for you. Not sold in stores. No capital or experience required. Write
J. W. HEITJAN, Gen. Mgr., CHICAGO SHIRT COMPANY
124 Chicago Shirt Bldg., Chicago, Ill.

MINSTRELS Musical Comedies and Revues, with full instructions for staging. You can stage your own show with our books. Full line of plays, stage songs, crossfire, monologues, afterpieces, vaudeville acts and make-up. CATALOGUE FREE.
T. S. Denison & Co. 623 So. Wabash, Dept. 89, Chicago

Ask for **Horlick's** The ORIGINAL Malted Milk
Safe Milk
For Infants, Children, Invalids, Nursing Mothers
Avoid Imitations

The American Legion: Sponsor of International Good Will

(Continued from page 11)

ideas of us. We have formed ours from the movies and from the peons who come to work at our dirty jobs; they have picked up theirs from the lowest and most disorderly types of merchant sailors, miners, oil-well laborers and the like who roister up and down the streets of Mexican cities just as they roister up and down the streets of some of our own cities on occasion, until the police break the disturbance up with night-sticks.

One of the most important jobs which can be done for the mutual welfare of the United States and Mexico is to give each side of the border an understanding of what lies on the other side. The Americans of the better class—of the average class, to be more exact—going quietly about their business, celebrating reverently their national holidays, give the Mexicans a better conception of our people as a whole.

But the other class of Americans are bound to be numerous in Tampico, both because it is an oil town and because it is a seaport. And a couple of years ago one could hardly walk a block down a street in Tampico without being stopped by an American begging for money or a meal.

Many of these men were legitimately up against it, either by reason of hard luck or bad judgment. Many of them, on the other hand, were of the sort which try to panhandle along the New York waterfront until they are stopped by the police.

American organizations in Tampico were all spending an amount of money for the relief of legitimate cases of need, and were doing what they could to co-operate with the Mexican authorities to keep down the other sort. It was costing a good deal of money, and was not getting any appreciable results. No matter how much was done, there seemed to remain exactly as much to be done. And the native opinion of Americans was not being materially helped by the situation.

In March of 1923 Tampico Post of the Legion stepped in quietly and called a meeting of all American organizations which were doing any relief work in Tampico. The Legion men at that meeting laid before the others the situation as they all knew it only too well; and it invited them to participate in organizing an American United Charities. The organizations which joined the enterprise are the American Legion Auxiliary, The American Legion, Woman's Club, Catholic Woman's Association, Rotary Club, American Chamber of Commerce, and Oil Managers' Association.

The newly organized United Charities elected H. H. Fleishman, who is now commander of the Legion Post, to be president for its first annual term. The board of directors consists of one representative from each participating American organization. This year the president is the representative of another organization, but the secretary and the treasurer are both Legion men.

The United Charities made up a budget of funds which it estimated would be needed to carry it a year.

Then it proceeded to raise the sum, $6,000 (American), by more or less of a levy on American residents, after the well-known fashion of community chest drives and the like. The amount, by the way, is much less than the seven participating outfits were spending before.

Today begging on the streets by Americans has been absolutely eliminated. And the American bums are off the streets, too. The United Charities has taken care of these men. It gets jobs for those who want jobs, or who will keep them. It gives them lodging, if they need it, and provides them with meal tickets good at certain places on signature by the beneficiary. And if a man is simply in the situation where he needs a little money to put him back on his own feet, it lends him the money. If he will not take the money, the Mexican authorities deport him as an undesirable alien; the Charities sees to that.

The Charities keeps continually leased two hotel rooms which contain eight beds. It leases a small hospital ward with four beds in the Civil Hospital, a Mexican institution. The Charities furnished the ward and pays for services as they are used. American doctors furnish their services free as a contribution to the movement—so far no hospital cases have required nursing beyond that given by the floor nurses of the hospital—if special nurses should be needed, a method of providing them would be devised.

In its first year, from March of 1923 to March of 1924, the United Charities furnished over 1,500 meals. It sent back to the States ten families and twenty men. It buried two men, and took care of about twenty hospital cases.

That is one job of community work which The American Legion has done in this Mexican city. Another job, none the less commendable because it has its parallel in a good many American communities, has to do with the local troop of the Boy Scouts of America.

The Boy Scout troop of Tampico had died sometime before when the Legion turned its attention to the situation. But in February of 1924 the post reorganized the local troop with the minimum number allowable.

If a Boy Scout troop is an important factor in an American city, consider its importance in Tampico. For here are a good many youngsters of American parentage, many of whom have never been in the United States. Even if they have made occasional visits, these have little chance to influence the boys materially, because for the greater part of their lives they live in a foreign city, surrounded by foreign customs and foreign ideals.

Unless something is done to build up in these boys an understanding of the things which are their national heritage, they become less American than Mexican. Their point of view tends toward the Latin, and when they return to the United States later they are bound to be out of tune and to an extent out ·of sympathy with American institutions.

Scouting gives these boys a common interest and strengthens their bonds to their country. It builds up in them the tradition of fair play and good sportsmanship which is the characteristic of true American boydom. It gives them a standard of patriotism to measure by, and to that extent makes them so much better residents of Mexico, from the Mexican as well as from the American viewpoint.

What the Boy Scouts in the United States do, these American Boy Scouts in Tampico do, and do well. They practise the "do a good deed every day" as assiduously as the Scouts of the thousands of American cities and towns do, thanks to the supervision of the Legionnaires who are their sponsors. It is a work that is quite as important as any that Legion Posts the world over are doing, for it takes the boy at a time when he is most impressionable, when he is most likely to be a hero worshipper, and moulds him into the best type of citizen.

In seven months the Tampico troop of Boy Scouts has grown to fifty-two, all of them American boys. Mexican boys, of course, cannot belong because they cannot take the oath of allegiance to the American flag. But a number of Mexican boys are, by invitation, doing the scout work along with the American kids.

The hope of the post is that these youngsters, trained with the American scouts in Tampico, may serve as a nucleus for a separate organization. There is no Boy Scouts of Mexico, although the Boy Scout movement has national organizations in a great many countries. The Mexican-boys who are working with the Tampico troop, and their parents as well, are actively interested in the idea.

The Legion post of Tampico is actively fostering the idea, for the benefit it will be to Mexico. H. H. Fleishman, P. B. Holsinger, and Mr. Berdie, who came from Tampico to the Saint Paul convention of the Legion, were in touch with Boy Scout officials during their trip in their effort to help the Mexicans organize.

At the outset, the Legion invited other organizations to participate with it in reviving and fostering the Tampico scout troop. But scouting is very close to the Legion heart, and Legion ideals, too. The outside organizations have definitely turned over the troop to Tampico Post now, and the resignations of their representatives—turned in in the best of spirit, for what the "outsiders" feel is the good of the troop—are being accepted one by one as Legionnaires are found to take over the responsibility.

Tampico Post publishes the *Foreign Legionnaire*, which is issued twice a month and sent to every American service man in Mexico of whom the post has record. The paper also is mailed regularly to all national officers of the Legion in the United States. It is a peppy little paper and serves to keep Legionnaires in Mexico as well as potential Legionnaires in touch with developments of American interest in that country.

There are seven posts of the Legion in Mexico—at Tampico, Mexico City, San Luis, Monterey, Chihuahua, Mata Redonda and Vera Cruz. All of them are engaged in strengthening, to the best of their abilities, the bond between the countries of their residence and of their birth. All of them are working for the good of the Americans in their vicinities. And all of them are making their communities better places to live in, for Mexicans and Americans alike.

A Legion Home That Pays Its Own Way

A dance hall, 35 feet by 75 feet, in the basement of this $22,000 Memorial Clubhouse of McKinley Post of Sebring, Ohio, has become the winter social center of the town. Revenue from dances given by the post meet all the expenses of maintaining the clubhouse

How to Get a Position with the U. S. Government

Thousands of appointments are made yearly. Good salaries—short hours—liberal vacations (as much as 30 days in some branches of the service). Positions open now in Washington and in other cities.

"Pull" and influence unnecessary. Common school education sufficient as groundwork for most positions. The International Correspondence Schools will prepare you right at home to pass your Civil Service examination with a high mark.

Mail the coupon today for 48-page Free Civil Service booklet.

INTERNATIONAL CORRESPONDENCE SCHOOLS
Box 7058-K, Scranton, Penna.
Without cost or obligation, please send me a copy of your 48-page CIVIL SERVICE BOOKLET, which tells how I can secure a good-paying position with the U. S. Government.

Name..

Address..

AGENTS SPARK PLUG NEW
Visible Flash

Just Out—Amazing Invention—Beacon Lite Spark Plugs. You see the flash of each explosion in the cylinders. This which are firing right. Greatest improvement in spark plugs since gas engines were invented. Wonderful gas savers. Agents coining money.

$90 A WEEK

Easy to make with new sure-fire plans. Sells on sight to every auto owner. Phillips, Ont., writes "Sold 2 dozen today, 3 dozen yesterday. Rush 10 dozen." Write for special Free Demonstrator Offer and FREE deal to introduce these wonder spark plugs in your territory. Write quick—today.

CENTRAL PETROLEUM COMPANY
511 Century Building   Cleveland, Ohio

Japanese Rose Bushes
Five for 10c

The Wonder of the World
Rose Bushes with roses on them in 8 weeks from the time the seed was planted. It may not seem possible but we Guarantee it to does. They will BLOOM EVERY TEN WEEKS Winter or Summer and when 3 years old will have 5 or 6 hundred roses on each bush. Will grow in the house in the winter as well as in the ground in summer. Roses All The Year Around. Pkgs. of Seed with our guarantee only 10c.

Japan Seed Co., Desk, 491   Norwalk, Conn.

PATENTS
Secured. Trademarks and Copyrights registered

E. E. STEVENS, Jr. Registered Patent Attorney Late of the 115th U. S. Infty.
LEGIONNAIRE OF MARYLAND
Solicits as a member of the old established firm of MILO B. STEVENS & CO., the business of his fellow Legionnaires and of their friends. We offer a strictly professional service at moderate fees. Preliminary advice without charge. Send sketch or model for examination. Offices, Barrister Bldg., Washington, D. C.; 838 Monadnock Block, Chicago, Ill.; Leader Building, Cleveland.

$15 a Day

We want men and women everywhere as local representatives to demonstrate and take orders for Comer All-Weather Coats. New offer enables you to earn $100 a week and a Dodge Touring Car. No capital, experience or training needed. Write for details.

THE COMER MFG. CO.
Dept. F-459   Dayton, Ohio

DODGE TOURING CAR   FREE

Bursts *and* Duds

Payment is made for material for this department. Unavailable manuscript returned only when accompanied by stamped envelope. Address American Legion Weekly, Indianapolis, Ind.

Company Coming

Butler: "And how many people will there be for dinner, sir?"

Master: "Four small glasses, two medium-sized and four extra large."

Eternal Punishment

A rich plumber who passed away and went where all plumbers go reported to the devil and was told to go ahead and install the new hot water system.

"All right," answered the plumber. "Give me a helper and I'll start in."

"Oh, you'll have to do the work yourself," chuckled Satan. "You don't have a helper. That's the hell of it."

A Puzzler

"What makes you seem so worried today, dear?" asked the professor's wife.

"I can't remember," he replied (for, strange to say, he was absent-minded), "which of the twins' birthdays is tomorrow."

Preparedness

"Now, if you're going to overcharge me," said the testy old lady to the taxi driver, "I wish you would tell me now, so that I can think up what I'm going to say to you."

Contrary

"An' yo' say dat little twin baby am a gal?" inquired Parson Jones of one of his colored flock.

"Yassuh."

"An' de other one. Am dat of de contrary sex?"

"Yassuh. She am a gal, too."

Use Discretion

"If you must shoot at a bear, George," implored the wife as her husband started on a hunting trip, "I do wish you would exercise a little common sense and shoot at one with a pleasant disposition and short legs.

Limerick

A clever young chap from **N. Y.**
Made oodles of money in **P.**
While out in **Wisc.**
He married Miss **J.**,
And now they're expecting the **st.**
—*J. O.*

Patent Applied For

Betty: "Mother, Bobbie is making a face at me."

Mother: "Well, don't pay any attention to him."

Betty: "Yes, but it's the kind of a face I invented."

Broadcasting: 3 A. M.

Station WIFE: "You poor, low-down, miserable excuse for a human being in the form of a man, where have you been?"

Station HUB: "Playin' poker down to

Jerry Canfield's, an' I win one hundred and twenty-four dollars, what I mean!"

Station WIFE: "Come right in, sweetheart."

No, Indeed

Newwed: "I insured my life for ten thousand dollars today, dear, so if anything happens to me, you'll be well provided for."

His Bride: "Oh, how nice! Now you won't have to see the doctor about your cough."

Officer: "Here, this isn't your birth certificate. It's your marriage license. Reasons for enlisting come last."

Down to Fine Points

"Man, ef Ah didn' have no mo' brains dan what yo' got, Ah'd—"

"Hesh up, boy! Ef yo' brains was dinamite, an' dey doubled ever' second for a honnerd yeahs an' den 'sploded, dey wouldn' blow yo' hat off on a windy day."

Overseas

Mary had a pot of ale,
And then some half-and-half,
But Mary lived in London town,
So where's the bloomin' laugh?
—*J. P. R.*

Outstanding

"Now," said the professor in the English history class just after he had described the battle of Hastings, "what is the next important date?"

"With Edith Wednesday afternoon," answered the student who had just waked up on the back seat.

Altruism

It was the year 2024. The United States had just elected its first woman President.

"Don't you feel that your home life will be ruined?" the Inquiring Reporter asked her husband.

"My only regret," he said with a sigh, "is that I have but one wife to give to my country."

Going the Route

A Southern land owner was returning home late one night when he was startled to see, in the bright moonlight, a disheveled looking negro come at top speed down the road.

"Here, stop a minute, what's the trouble?" he demanded. "You seem mighty scared."

"Ah is skeered," replied the colored one, slackening his speed somewhat. "Ah seed a ghos' down to de graveyard."

"But you're running toward the graveyard now, instead of away from it."

"Ah knows dat, suh, but de graveyard Ah is runnin' f'om am fo' counties back."

Cheap Labor

Blake: "We ought to ask the bishop to lay the cornerstone of our new building."

Drake: "Yes, we'll save money if we can get him to do it instead of the bricklayers."

Rotten

Junior Partner: "Well, how's business?"

Senior Partner: "Absolutely gone to the devil. Why, do you know this is the first month for thirty-seven months we have failed to beat all previous months' production records?"

The Age of Luxury

[*From the Vicksburg (Miss.), Evening Post*]

FOR RENT—Furnished front room with garage, 913 Jackson, across street from post-office.

Not Quite

"If I had refused you, darling," murmured the romantic maiden, "would you have driven your car over the brink of the precipice, dashing us both into eternity, like the lover we saw in the movie the other night?"

"N-no, not this car, honey," answered the practical and truthful swain. "You see, I've just had new tires put on all the way 'round."

The Age of Speed

"I want to tell you, young feller," began the old timer, "that when I was your age I had to work twelve hours a day."

"Huh! You couldn't get away with that now," sneered the young squirt. "They'd fire a guy who couldn't do his stuff faster'n that."

Suspicious

"Now I don't want you to go to any trouble on my account," politely announced the missionary who had dropped around at mealtime.

"We won't," grimly announced the cannibal chief. "You'll have to take pot luck."

THE GREATEST WAR HISTORY OF ALL TIME

All the Overseas Issues of
The Stars and Stripes

IN ONE COMPLETE ART LEATHER BOUND VOLUME

IN this complete, bound volume of the overseas issues of "The Stars and Stripes" there is, indeed, the greatest and most complete war history ever published—Why?—Because it is the vivid, gripping story of the A. E. F., told in a way that only men "who got there" could tell it. A complete file of the overseas "Stars and Stripes" is real history—the War—live and virile. Pathos of the sort that grips your throat and blurs your eyes. Humor of the sort that forces smiles from even dignified Major-Generals.

So complete and accurate is the overseas "Stars and Stripes" that you can write a complete service record of every Division and branch of the Service from its pages. What did your Division do? What did your branch of the service do? You will find the answer—a true, authentic answer written by the men on the spot—in this wonderful volume.

Who can better describe war-time France, and the battlefields, than the man in the O. D. Jeans?

A COMPLETE HISTORY
of Every Division and Branch of the Service

THE overseas issues of "The Stars and Stripes" make an ideal gift. It is a gift that will grow in value as the years roll on. The reprinted bound file of "The Stars and Stripes" is exactly like the original, word for word, line for line. In all, there are 71 issues. Each issue was an 8-page newspaper, 18½ inches by 24½ inches in size. All 71 issues are beautifully bound in an art leather volume that will last for years.

For the man who was "over there" a glance at the pages of the old "Stars and Stripes" is like a round trip ticket to yesterday—a passport back to the A. E. F. It is a gold mine of recollections. An unequaled remembrance to the most thrilling days of your life.

Here alone can you find accounts of the little incidents which make The Stars and Stripes different from any publication you have ever seen before.

only a few copies left ORDER NOW

Priceless Souvenir of the War

SEND ONLY $1

A complete file of The Stars and Stripes is a priceless souvenir. For the man who was there, it is a gold mine of recollections—an unequaled remembrance of the finest days of his life. Once you get your hands on this amazing file, you'll stay with it until long after taps.

The Legion Book Service has been fortunate in securing the few copies that are available and we are offering them to our readers at a price lower than the file has ever been sold for. Orders will be filled in sequence received. Take advantage of our special offer today. Mail in the coupon attached to this ad and assure yourself of getting a copy.

THE LEGION BOOK SERVICE, DEPT. S,
of
THE AMERICAN LEGION WEEKLY,
Indianapolis, Indiana.

I enclose $1.00 deposit in good faith. Send me, all charges prepaid, a complete bound file of the overseas "Stars and Stripes," bound in dark green leather. I agree upon delivery of the volume to pay the mailman $9.00, plus a few cents postage fees, the balance of your special reduced price. It is understood that this is in no way to be considered a purchase. If at the end of 5 days I am not completely satisfied, I am to have the privilege of returning the volume to you at your expense and you will refund all my money.

Name _____

Street _____

City _____

State _____

New Way to Grow Hair

—But Here's POSITIVE PROOF of What I Am Doing Everywhere

These are true letters sent me by some of the thousands of people who have taken my remarkable new treatment for baldness and falling hair. These are not rare instances. Enthusiastic letters are pouring in daily telling of the astonishing results being secured everywhere—through use of my scientific system. What better proof is there that I can *actually grow new hair?* To try my new discovery you need not risk a cent. For I positively *guarantee* results or charge you nothing. Mail the coupon for free booklet describing my system and 30 Day Trial offer in detail.

By ALOIS MERKE
Founder of Famous Merke Institute
Fifth Avenue, New York

Who Else Wants a New Head of Hair Like This?

A NEW growth of hair in 30 Days—or no cost! This may sound impossible to you. But just read the statements from users of my method printed on this page. These are true excerpts from original letters and are typical of hundreds of others in our files which are open at all times to the inspection of any one interested.

I don't say my system will grow hair for everyone. There are some cases of baldness that nothing in the world can help. But I've grown new hair for so many thousands of others who had given up hope that I am entirely willing to let you try it at my risk for 30 Days. Then, no matter how fast you are losing your hair—no matter how little of it there is now left—if you are not more than delighted with the growth of hair produced I will instantly and gladly mail you a check refunding every cent you have paid me. That's my absolute GUARANTEE, AND YOU ARE THE SOLE JUDGE. I take all the risk. You take none whatever.

Entirely New System

Most people believe that when their hair falls out the roots are dead. But I have proven that in the majority of cases the hair roots are merely dormant—inactive. Through under-nourishment, dandruff and other causes the starving, shrunken hair roots have literally gone into a state of "suspended animation."

Tonics, ointments, massages, crude oil, etc., etc., fail to grow new hair because they do not *reach* these *dormant* hair roots, but instead simply treat the surface of the scalp. To make a tree grow you would not rub "growing fluid" on the bark. Instead you would get right to the roots. And so it is with the hair. My new method provides an effective way of properly treating dormant hair roots and stimulating them into a new and natural growth. And the fine thing about my system is the fact that it is *simple* and *inexpensive* and can be used in any home where there is electricity, without the slightest *discomfort* or *inconvenience.*

Mail Coupon Now

The very fact that you have read this announcement shows that you are anxious about the condition of your hair. So why not investigate? Find out for yourself. That's the only common-sense thing to do. If you will merely fill in and mail the coupon below I will gladly send you, without cost or obligation, a wonderfully interesting booklet which describes in detail my successful system which is growing new hair on happy heads all over the country. Clip and mail the coupon today. Allied Merke Institutes, Inc., Dept. 221, 512 Fifth Ave., New York City.

Read These Letters!

New Hair Growing
"Results are wonderful. My hair has stopped falling out and I can see lots of new hair coming in."—F. D. R., Washington, D. C.

New Hair on Bald Spots
"I have used Thermocap Treatment for 8 weeks and, although the top of my head has been entirely bald for 6 years, the results up to the present are gratifying. In fact, the entire bald spot is covered with a fine growth of hair."—W. C. Kenmore, Ohio.

Can't Say Enough For It
"Am glad to say I can see such great change in my hair. It is growing longer and my head is full of young hair that has made its way through since I have been using Merke Thermocap. I can't say enough for it. It will do everything you claim it to do."—G. G., Texas.

Results Gratifying
"Ten years ago my hair started falling. I used hair tonics constantly but four years ago I displayed a perfect full moon. I tried everything—but without results. Today, however, thanks to your treatment, I have quite a new crop of hair one inch long."—F. H. B., New York.

Hair About Gone
"My hair had been falling for the last two years and I had hardly any more hair on the front of my head. But since I started using your treatment I am raising a new crop of hair. Your treatment is best I ever saw."—O. J., Northbridge, Mass.

Falling Hair Checked
"My hair was coming out at an alarming rate, but after four or five treatments I noticed this was checked. My hair is coming in thicker and looks and feels full of life and vigor."—W. C., Great Neck, L. I.

NOTE These testimonials used in connection with the Merke Thermocap Treatment are true extracts from original letters on file in the Allied Merke Institutes, which files are open to the inspection of anyone interested, at all times. Many other letters will be sent with your free booklet, together with affidavit certifying to them.

The New Way to Make Hair Grow

Get This Book

ALLIED MERKE INSTITUTES, Inc., Dept. 221, 512 Fifth Avenue, New York City.

Please send me—without cost or obligation—a copy of your book describing the Merke System.

Name _____
(State whether Mr., Mrs. or Miss)

Address _____

City _____ State _____

CPSIA information can be obtained
at www.ICGtesting.com
Printed in the USA
BVHW041120211218
536175BV00005B/19/P

9 780483 956681